Disney
HANNAH MONTANA

Hannah's
HANG-OUT
GUIDE

©2007 Disney.

Modern Publishing
A Division of Unisystems, Inc.
New York, New York 10022
Printed in India
Series UPC: 65085

BASED ON THE TELEVISION SERIES "HANNAH MONTANA", CREATED BY MICHAEL PORYES AND RICH CORRELL & BARRY O'BRIEN

Hannah's HANG-OUT BASICS!

TOP TIPS

DON'T OVER-INVITE! Sure, it would be kind of cool to have the whole school at your party. But, do you really know everyone that well? If there are too many people at your party, you won't be able to spend enough time with your close friends.

BE SURE TO HAVE ENOUGH FOOD AND DRINKS to last the whole party! There's nothing worse than running out of something that's a hit and having to run out in the middle of your get-together to buy more!

SET UP A PLAYLIST OR BURN A CD of the hottest new songs before the party-it's WAY better than having to scan through the radio to find a station playing a good song!

PARTY CHECKLIST

To be the host with the most, you have to be organized!
Use this checklist while you plan and prepare for your party!

_____ PLAN GUEST LIST

_____ WRITE OUT INVITATIONS

_____ SEND AND HAND OUT INVITATIONS

_____ PLAN MENU

_____ BUY FOOD/SNACKS/DRINKS

_____ PLAN DECORATIONS

_____ BUY DECORATIONS AND PARTY GOODS

_____ PLAN PARTY GAMES

_____ PLAN PARTY MUSIC PLAYLIST

_____ HAVE HANNAH MONTANA DVD READY

_____ HAVE HANNAH MONTANA SOUNDTRACK
ON HAND

Hannah's HANG-OUT PARTY THEMES

Sure, you can have a good old-fashioned afternoon hang-out with the girls or a simple get-together. Those are always fun! But if you want to make your party unique, try one of these fun themes that are favorites of Miley and Lilly!

SLAMMIN' SLEEPOVER!

Tell the girls to pack their PJs—it's time for a slammin' sleepover! Here are some fun ideas for a sweet slumber party:

Catch up on your crushes! Since the sleepover will be girls only, what better time to rate your crushes, compare notes and reveal your newest secret crush!

Have a pajama fashion show! Set up a runway, and strut your stuff! Give out prizes for coolest, funniest, and weirdest PJs!

Do blindfolded makeovers! One person puts a blindfold over her eyes and applies lipstick, eye shadow and blush to a brave victim. Take pictures—these are memories you won't want to forget!

SOOTHING SPA!

Set up a soothing spa and pamper yourselves! Here are some ideas:

Set up different stations: nail polish, cotton puffs and nail polish remover for a manicure/pedicure station. Put out cucumber slices (for your eyes), ice water with slices of fruit in it and soothing music for a relaxation station. Set up handheld massagers for a massage station!

Make some Spa Smoothies! Blend some plain yogurt or ice cream with fresh berries!

BERRY BLITZ

YOU'LL NEED:
1/2 cup of ripe strawberries
1/4 cup of cornstarch

MIX IT UP:
1. Mash strawberries and cornstarch together to make a paste.
2. Apply to your face—leave on for 30 minutes.
3. Rinse off with cool water.

POP STAR KARAOKE!

How perfect for a Hannah Montana Hang Out! Grab your microphone and reveal your inner pop star:

Each girl takes a turn singing the Hannah Montana theme song! Give out prizes for best performance, most like Hannah, and most out-there.

Pick your favorite song from the Hannah Montana soundtrack and re-write the lyrics so they're about you and your friends. Perform it for the girls.

Have fun dancing and singing your fave Hannah tunes!

SECRET STAR COSTUME PARTY

Are you a totally true-blue Hannah Montana fan? Then this is THE party theme for you.

On your invitations, add a note telling your friends to come to the party dressed as their favorite Hannah Montana character!

Give out prizes for the best costume!

Hannah's SNACK SHACK!

POP STAR PARTY PUNCH
Go glam with this fizzy party punch!

YOU'LL NEED:
2 cups fruit juice
1 6-ounce can frozen juice concentrate
1 liter seltzer
HINT: Stick to the same fruit flavor for the juice, concentrate and seltzer (or you can use plain seltzer).

Pour the fruit juice and concentrate into a pitcher and mix well. Chill it overnight. Right before you serve it, pour the seltzer into the juice mix. Serve over crushed ice.

DRESSED-UP PRETZEL STICKS
Plain old pretzels? No way—try these!

YOU'LL NEED:
Pretzel rods
Peanut butter
Chocolate chips

Dip a pretzel stick in peanut butter.
Roll the pretzel in chocolate chips. Yummy!

Want to really impress your party guests?
Try out some of these
awesome (and easy)
party snack recipes!

POPCORN BALLS

Try this new twist on an old favorite!

YOU'LL NEED:
2 cups granulated sugar
1 cup light corn syrup
1 cup water
3 tbsp. butter
2 quarts popped popcorn

Ask an adult to help. Mix all ingredients in a pot, except popcorn, and cook on medium heat until melted(until the mixture bubbles). Pour over salted popcorn. Mix thoroughly and mold into balls.

DO-IT-YOURSELF
ICE-CREAM SUNDAE BAR

Get your friends in on the fun and let them make their own sundaes!

YOU'LL NEED:

Chocolate ice cream
Vanilla ice cream
Sprinkles
Chocolate chips

Chopped nuts
Hot fudge
Cherries
Whipped cream

Let everyone create their own ice-cream sensation. Be sure to set out plenty of napkins!

DOUBLE AS A SUPERSTAR!

Try this twist on charades! Each player takes a turn acting out part of an episode of Hannah Montana. It can be anything—a dance, a song, a conversation. There's a catch (of course)! You can't actually speak or sing, you have to act it out. But, don't make the game TOO hard (otherwise it won't be fun). Before you take your turn, tell your players if they should be guessing a song, a character or scene from the show.

PARTY GAMES!

TAKE TWO!

Pop your Hannah Montana DVD into the DVD player. Ask one person to stop the episode at a random scene. The first player has to pick up where that scene leaves off and finish the scene. If they don't know the next line, they have to make it up! The person who can finish the most scenes wins. (But, you'll have lots of laughs at the made-up scenes!)

PICTURE THIS!

You know everything there is to know about Hannah Montana, right? Put your expertise to the test! Split up into two teams. Pick a scene a character, a place—anything—from the show. Draw it, or draw clues that will help the players guess what you're drawing. The first team to get **10** points wins!

REVEAL YOUR SECRET SELF!

Before the party, prepare special candy bags. In clear baggies, put candies of the following colors (you can use hard candies, gum, candy-coated chocolate, lollipops, etc): yellow, blue, red, green, purple, orange. (One color per-bag don't mix the colors.) Then, in one bowl, place all the red, blue and yellow bags. In a separate bowl, place all the green, orange and purple bags. Ask each guest to pick ONE bag from each bowl. Then check out the results to see what your choices say about you!

 Red/Green:
You're calm and level-headed!

 Red/Purple:
You're at your best when you're in control!

 Red/Orange:
You are a true individual. You, follow the crowd? Never!

 Yellow/Green:
You are a great listener and friends come to you for advice!

 Yellow/Purple:
You love adventure and trying new things!

 Yellow/Orange:
You LOVE a challenge and you HATE routine!

 Blue/Green:
You're really curious and super observant!

 Blue/Purple:
You love to be the center of attention (hello, Hannah!)!

 Blue/Orange:
You are unpredictable—free-spirited one minute and reserved the next!

PARTY GAMES!

SUPER SECRET PARTY PEOPLE PASS-ALONG BOOK

At your party, create a Super Secret Pass-Along Book (Party People Edition)! Get a blank notebook. On the first page, write down everyone's name on a numbered list (your name goes first). You start the first entry—write ANYTHING you want: thoughts, secrets, questions for your friends to answer, requests for your friends, pictures, etc. Then, pass the journal to the #2 person on the list, and then she passes it on when she's done, and so on! You can keep the journal going forever—long after the party's over!

WOULD U RATHER...

This is a fun game to get to know things about your best friends that you would never have guessed! Ask the questions and start the laughs!

WOULD YOU RATHER BE A POP STAR OR A RUNWAY MODEL?

WOULD YOU RATHER BE SUPER FAMOUS OR SUPER SMART?

WOULD YOU RATHER HAVE FIVE SISTERS OR FIVE BROTHERS?

WOULD YOU RATHER BE INVISIBLE OR BE ABLE TO FLY?

WOULD YOU RATHER PLAY SPORTS OR WATCH SPORTS?

WOULD YOU RATHER HAVE A REALLY BAD HAIRCUT OR BE WEARING A REALLY HIDEOUS OUTFIT?

WOULD YOU RATHER BE HANNAH OR MILEY?

WOULD YOU RATHER BE LILLY OR MILEY?

WOULD YOU RATHER DATE OLIVER OR JACKSON?

WOULD YOU RATHER BE GROUNDED FOR A MONTH OR NOT ALLOWED TO SHOP FOR SIX MONTHS?

WOULD YOU RATHER GO SWIMMING OR ICE SKATING?

WOULD YOU RATHER HAVE LOTS OF FRIENDS WHO DON'T KNOW YOU THAT WELL OR ONE REALLY GOOD FRIEND WHO KNOWS YOU INSIDE AND OUT?

WHO'S YOUR HANNAH MONTANA TWIN?

1. What are you most likely to be wearing on a Saturday?
a. A sparkly tank top and jeans
b. A cute pink sweater and a jean skirt
c. A pair of board shorts and a t-shirt

2. A perfect night of fun for you involves:
a. Hitting the town—where you can be seen
b. Watching a movie with your best friend
c. Skateboarding

3. At a party, you are the girl:
a. In the middle of the crowd, talking away
b. Hanging out with a small group of your closest friends
c. Saying something silly

4. Your favorite color is:
a. Red
b. Pink
c. Orange

5. In a friendship you are the one who:
a. Is usually in the spotlight
b. Is usually the voice of reason
c. Is there whenever your friend needs you

If you answered:
MOSTLY A's: You are a HANNAH CLONE! You like to be the center of attention and the life of the party!
MOSTLY B's: You are MOST LIKE MILEY! You like to hang out with your closest friends and stay low key!
MOSTLY C's: You are a LOT LIKE LILLY! You are into sports and love to just chill with your friends!

WHAT'S YOUR FRIEND FACTOR?

Give yourself one point for each true answer:

I am there for my friends whenever they need me—day or night! TRUE or FALSE
I would skip a party if my friend needed me for something! TRUE or FALSE
My friends are allowed to borrow any of my clothes! TRUE or FALSE
I am the person that my friends usually go to for advice! TRUE or FALSE
I know my friends like the back of my hand! TRUE or FALSE
I would never lie to my friends. TRUE or FALSE
I would defend my friend if I ever heard anyone talk about her. TRUE or FALSE
I love spending time with my friends! TRUE or FALSE
My friends come first (before my crush)! TRUE or FALSE
I never let my friends' secrets out of the bag! TRUE or FALSE

1-3 TRUE: You need to be a little less selfish in order to become a better friend!
4-6 TRUE: You're a pretty good friend, but you could still use some improvement!
7-10 TRUE: You are a girl's best friend! You have what it takes to be a friend for life!

POP QUIZZES!

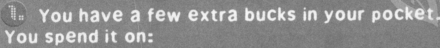

1. You have a few extra bucks in your pocket. You spend it on:

a. Stuff from the craft store—there are some gifts you've been meaning to make for your friends
b. A new headband
c. Renting the latest DVD

2. So many magazines, so little time. You pick:

a. A decorating mag
b. A fashion mag
c. A gossip mag

3. The first thing you notice in someone's room is:

a. The color of the walls
b. The pattern on the curtains
c. The pictures or posters

4. You need a new scarf. You:

a. Find a cool fabric and make it yourself
b. Buy a scarf that has the trendiest new pattern on it
c. Try to find a scarf just like the one you saw on your fave movie star in her latest flick

5. The word people would use to describe you is:

a. Creative
b. Trendy
c. Superstar

If you answered:

MOSTLY A's: You are an UNDERCOVER ARTIST! Whether it's crafts, interior decorating or painting you have a real talent when it comes to being creative!

MOSTLY B's: You are an UNDERCOVER FASHION DESIGNER! You are up on the latest trends and definitely have an eye for fashion!

MOSTLY C's: You are an UNDERCOVER CELEBRITY! You could totally be a movie star, singing sensation or even an entertainment reporter!

Hannah	Miley
Lilly	Mitchel
Lola	Jason
Oliver	Billy Ray
Jackson	Rico's Surf Shop
Roxy	Beach
Rico	Secret
Jake	Montana
Robbie	Stewart
Cooper	Truscott
Amber	Oken
Ashley	Pop Star
Superstar	Concert
Smokin' Oken	Friends
Malibu	Music
Emily	

Hannah Montana BINGO!

HERE'S A FUN GAME TO PLAY AT YOUR PARTY!

1. Cut out the Bingo cards on the following pages.

2. Cut out all of the names on this page and put them in a bowl or a bag.

3. One person is the caller. That person picks a slip of paper from the bowl and reads it.

4. Everyone checks out his or her Bingo card. If the word called is on your card (or if a photo of the character whose name was called is on your card), place a coin or a button on that space. (Don't forget to mark off your free space at the beginning of the game!)

5. The game goes on until someone fills up a row across, up and down, horizontally, or diagonally and yells "Bingo!"

Pop Star	Secret	Smokin' Oken		Friends
Oken	Billy Ray	Stewart	Ashley	
Beach	Rico's Surf Shop	FREE	Truscott	
Jason		Music	Friends	Emily
Montana	Roxy		Cooper	Concert

	Malibu	Billy Ray	Pop Star	Rico's Surf Shop
Roxy	Secret	Mitchel	Stewart	Jason
Beach	Amber	FREE		
Montana	Concert		Cooper	Emily
Music		Truscott	Rico	Jake

Card 1

Truscott	Rico	Smokin' Oken	Oken	Lola
	Roxy	Montana	Malibu	Emily
Jake		FREE	Jason	Secret
Cooper	Beach	Concert		Pop Star
Superstar	Jason		Music	Friends

Card 2

	Beach	Pop Star		Superstar
	Malibu	Truscott	Smokin' Oken	Rico
Montana	Billy Ray	FREE	Friends	
Amber	Lola		Billy Ray	Stewart
Ashley		Music	Rico	Secret

WHO'S WHO?

Press out the cards. Mix them up and turn them face down. One player picks a card without revealing it to anyone else. Then by giving one word clues, that player tries to get everyone else to guess what's on his or her card! The player who guesses correctly is the next player up! The catch—the clues cannot be the name of the character and the harder the clues, the harder it will be for anyone to beat you!

RICO		*Lola*
	**Amber**	
Ashley		**COOPER**
	**ROXY**	

Wheel of Hannah!

Follow the instructions to put your game together. Once it's assembled, one girl closes her eyes and turns the wheel. When she stops turning, she opens her eyes and checks out the character she landed on. Then she has to act like that character until someone can guess who she's imitating!

To Assemble:

1. Press out both wheels.

2. Press out the window and the middle of the top wheel.

3. Press up the 3 flaps in the center of the bottom disk.

4. Fold the flaps up and stick them through the center of the top wheel. Then flatten them.

GUEST LIST!

Who will you invite to your party?
Plan your guest list here! Wipe the page clean
and do the same for your next get-together!

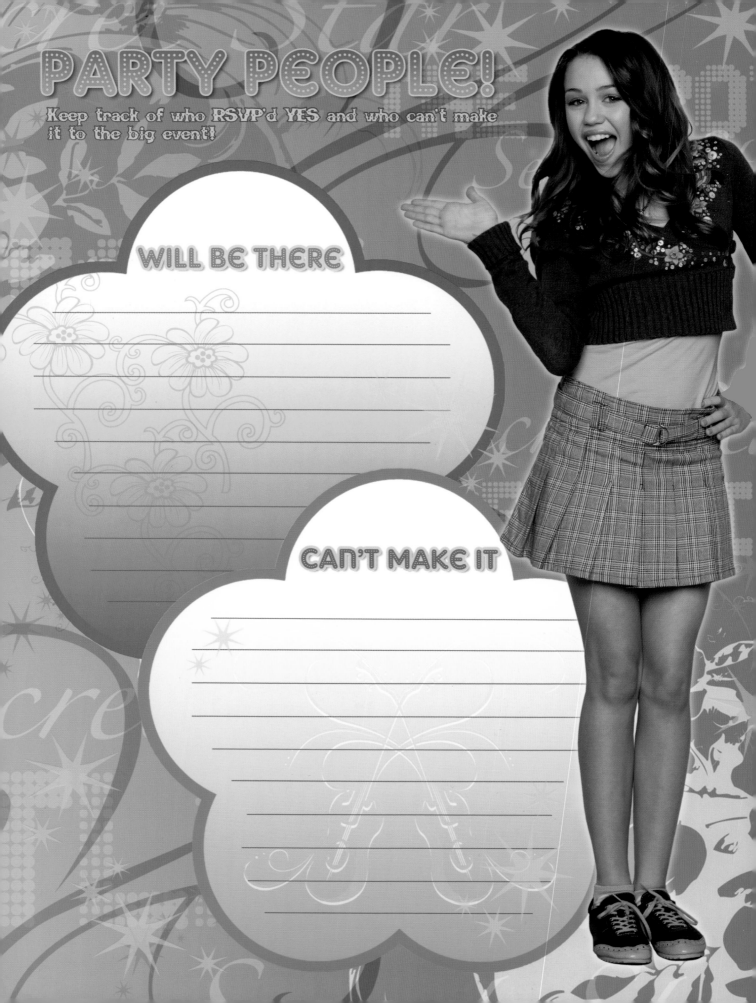

PARTY PEOPLE!

Keep track of who RSVP'd YES and who can't make it to the big event!

WILL BE THERE

CAN'T MAKE IT

HANNAH MONTANA

Put Me in the Spotlight

PUT ME IN TH

PARTY NOTES!

Cut out these fun notes along the dotted lines. Then fold along the solid lines.
Write a message inside thanking your guest for coming to your party,
seal with a sticker, and hand them out!

HANNAH PARTY FAVOR FRAMES!

Cut out your frames. Paste a picture from the party in each one and give them out to your friends!

Lola

Rico

What would people be surprised to learn about you?

Would you rather be the normal girl-next-door or an on-the-go superstar? Why?

Jackson

Montana

Who would you rather date – Oliver or Jackson? Why?

Sing your favorite Hannah Montana Song right now!

What would your stage name be?

What is your most secret wish?

Miley

Oliver

If you could be famous for anything, what would it be?

Tell your crush he looks cute today!

5

Hannah

Lilly

6

How To Play:

1. Ask a friend to pick a number from one of the outside flaps. Open and close your fingers that number of times (moving your fingers back and forth and the sideways).

2. Have your friend choose one of the words on the inside. Spell out the word, opening and closing your fingers with each letter.

3. Have your friend pick one of the words shown. Open that flap and read the message!

How To Fold:

1. Cut out the square along the dotted lines. Fold and unfold it in half diagonally in both directions to make an X. Then place the square question-side down.

2. Fold each corner point into the center.

3. Flip so that the flaps are facedown. Then fold each corner into the center.

4. Fold in half, from top to bottom.

5. Then unfold and fold in half, from side to side.

6. Stick both thumbs and index fingers into the four pockets. Index fingers go in the front pockets and thumbs go in the back pockets. Push all the pockets to a point.

BEST PARTY EVER!

TAPE PICTURE HERE

_____
_____
was the person
who looked most
like a secret
superstar!

TAPE PICTURE HERE

The best game
played was
_____
_____
_____
_____
_____ !

The funnniest
thing that happened at
the party was
_____
_____
_____
_____
_____
_____ !

TAPE PICTURE HERE

I'll always
remember this
party because
_____
_____
_____
_____
_____ !

TAPE PICTURE HERE

TAPE PICTURE HERE

WHICH CHARACTER ARE YOU MOST LIKE?

Set out a bunch of see-through baggies, each filled with different treat combos. Make sure that there are enough bags for each of your guests. Then ask everyone to pick the candy bag that they like most. Then, check out the list to see which character each person is most like! Have fun eating the rest of the treats!

Bag A

Gumdrops With Lots of Sparkly Sugar

Cookies with Tons of Sprinkles

Bag B

Jelly Beans

Cotton Candy

Bag C

Bubblegum

Rainbow Lollipops

IF YOU PICKED
BAG A
you're most like...

HANNAH!

You're totally glamorous and a natural superstar!

IF YOU PICKED
BAG B
you're most like...

MILEY!

You're a really sweet, down-to-earth, popular girl-next-door!

IF YOU PICKED
BAG C
you're most like...

LILLY!

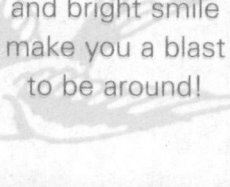

Your fun nature and bright smile make you a blast to be around!

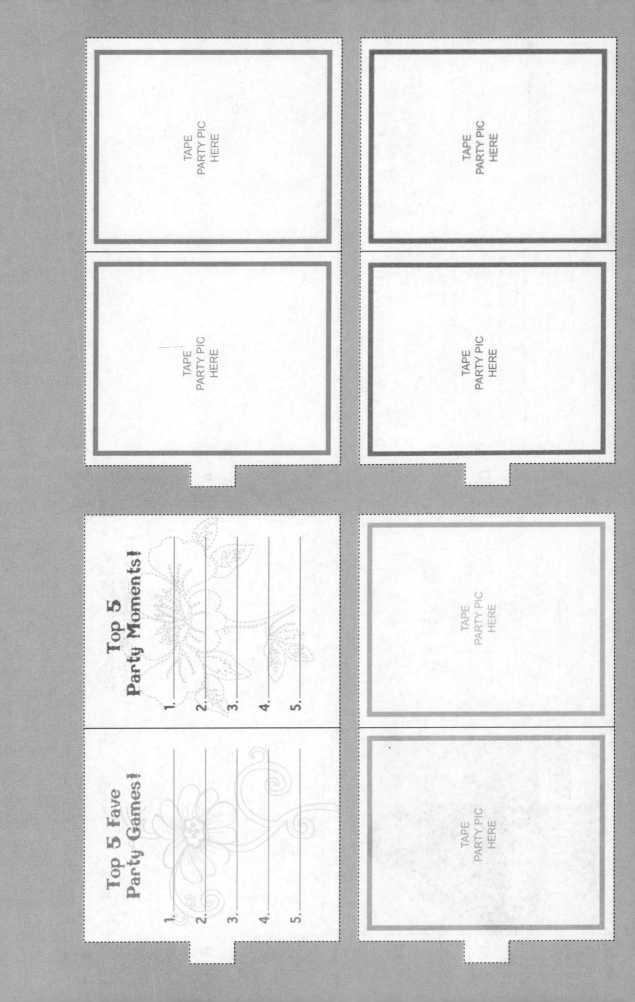

TAPE
PARTY PIC
HERE

TAPE
PARTY PIC
HERE

TAPE
PARTY PIC
HERE

TAPE
PARTY PIC
HERE

Top 5 Fave
Party Games!

1.
2.
3.
4.
5.

Top 5
Party Moments!

1.
2.
3.
4.
5.

TAPE
PARTY PIC
HERE

TAPE
PARTY PIC
HERE

PARTY TIME
MINI MAG!

FOLLOW THESE INSTRUCTIONS TO MAKE YOUR OWN PARTY TIME MINI MAG!

1. Cut out each set of pages along the dotted lines.

2. Make sure you cut around the tabs.

3. Stack the pages on top of each other, in the following order (from top to bottom): D, C, B, A. The letters on the tabs should be facing up.

4. Fold the stack of pages down the middle, along the solid line.

5. Cut the tabs off.

6. Have fun with your party guests putting the finishing touches on the mag!

5 Ideas For My Next Party!

1.
2.
3.
4.
5.

All About My Party

C

TAPE PARTY PIC HERE

TAPE PARTY PIC HERE

A

5 Reasons Why This Party Rocked!

1.
2.
3.
4.
5.

CREATED BY:

D

PARTY TIME MINI MAG!

Disney HANNAH MONTANA

Party Guests

B

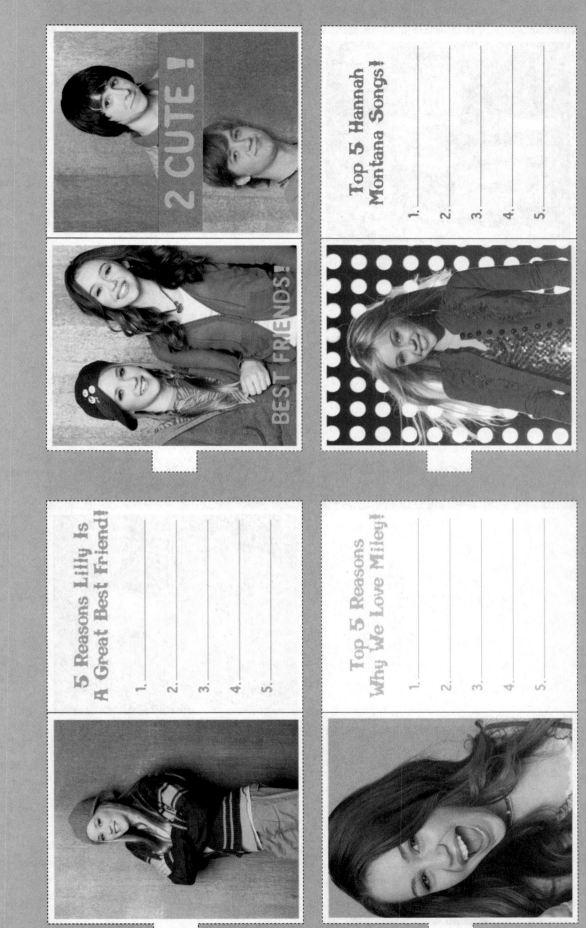

2 CUTE!

BEST FRIENDS!

Top 5 Hannah
Montana Songs!

1. _____
2. _____
3. _____
4. _____
5. _____

5 Reasons Lilly Is
A Great Best Friend!

1. _____
2. _____
3. _____
4. _____
5. _____

Top 5 Reasons
Why We Love Miley!

1. _____
2. _____
3. _____
4. _____
5. _____

FOLLOW THESE INSTRUCTIONS TO MAKE YOUR OWN HANNAH MONTANA MINI MAG!

1. Cut out each set of pages along the dotted lines.

2. Make sure you cut around the tabs.

3. Stack the pages on top of each other, in the following order (from top to bottom): D, C, B, A. The letters on the tabs should be facing up.

4. Fold the stack of pages down the middle, along the solid line.

5. Cut the tabs off.

6. Have fun with your party guests putting the finishing touches on the mag!

5 Reasons Why Jackson is a Cool Brother to Miley!

1. _____
2. _____
3. _____
4. _____
5. _____

A

5 Reasons Why Hannah Montana Is The Best Show Ever!

1. _____
2. _____
3. _____
4. _____
5. _____

C

5 Reasons We Love Oliver!

1. _____
2. _____
3. _____
4. _____
5. _____

B

CREATED BY:

_____
_____
_____
_____

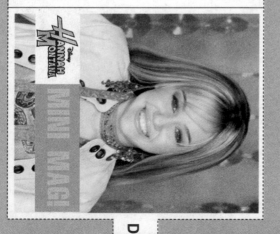

MINI MAG!

Disney HANNAH MONTANA

D

	Music	Rico's Surf Shop	Jason	
Roxy	Oken	Stewart	Truscott	Montana
Secret	Smokin' Oken	FREE		Emily
Billy Ray		Jake	Cooper	Superstar
	Friends	Concert	Lola	Jason

Secret		Lola	Truscott	Friends
Stewart	Concert	Oken	Roxy	Mitchel
	Music	FREE	Beach	Emily
Montana	Superstar	Amber		
	Pop Star	Jake	Rico	

Card 1

Jake	Beach	Cooper		Billy Ray
Amber	Pop Star	Secret	Rico's Surf Shop	Jason
Mitchel		FREE	Concert	Lola
Rico	Oken	Stewart		Montana
Ashley	Malibu	Roxy	Truscott	

Card 2

Concert		Roxy	Oken	Stewart
Beach		Jake	Billy Ray	Emily
Ashley		FREE	Secret	Amber
Emily		Pop Star	Friends	Mitchel
Superstar		Malibu	Music	Jason